THEORY OF ETHNICITY

An Anthropologist's Perspective

Ronald A. Reminick

UNIVERSITY
PRESS OF
AMERICA

LANHAM • NEW YORK • LONDON

University Press of America,™ Inc.

4720 Boston Way
Lanham, MD 20706

3 Henrietta Street
London WC2E 8LU England

Library of Congress Cataloging in Publication Data

Reminick, Ronald A.
    Theory of ethnicity.

    Bibliography: p.
    1. Ethnicity. 2. Pluralism (Social sciences) I. Title.
GN495.6.R45   1983   305.8   83–1161
ISBN 0–8191–3075–3
ISBN 0–8191–3076–1 (pbk.)

for
evelyn

Acknowledgements

My special thanks and appreciation are due my
colleagues, Professor Paul Aspelin and Professor
Leon Soulé, for their careful and critical
readings of the initial drafts of this manuscript.
My gratitude is extended to many of my students
whose conscientious work and responsive feedback to
the material herein has guided me in the selection
and organization of these ideas. I also extend my
thanks to the staff of the Cleveland State
University Word Processing Service who in no small
way facilitated subsequent revisions of this
manuscript.

TABLE OF CONTENTS

Preface

This work grew out of a course in urban ethnic cultures developed for the general interest of university students. In exploring the characteristics of specific ethnic groups I felt a strong need to accompany that data with some form of unifying framework. Further, I wanted this framework to be eclectic, ideally a synthesis of concepts and theories representing a cross section of the behavioral sciences. I found virtually no literature to approach the kind of book I had in mind. This particular book goes a long way in satisfying the goals I had in providing my students with a theoretical and orientational framework for thinking about and perceiving the personal qualities and shared group features of particular ethnic persons and groups and their ethnic cultures. This book examines the concept of ethnicity from a systems-oriented perspective utilizing concepts and theories that are widely dispersed in the literature and reorganized and reintegrated within an anthropological framework. As such, this book can be used by students as a supplement to specific ethnographies and ethnic studies dealing with the ethnic cultures of particular peoples, most appropriately found within the American context.

INTRODUCTION

The objective of this study is to summarize and organize major theoretical ideas from the several social science disciplines in an attempt to generate a more coherent system of general theoretical ideas that function to explain the nature of ethnicity, its roles both as a conservative force and as an agent of change in the dynamics of modern urban society. The organization of this information is divided into two parts: Part I includes the elaboration of the major concepts at three levels of operation: The social structural level attends to a) the place ethnicity occupies with the macrosocial structures and gemeinschaft structures of society; b) the primary components and the boundary-maintaining mechanisms of ethnic groups; and c) a comparative examination of selected definitions of the concept of ethnicity. At the cultural level of operation I give an elaborated definition of the concept of culture and point out the analytical similarities and differences between the general phenomenon of culture and the more particularized concept of ethnic culture. At the psychological level of operation I focus upon the problem of ethnic identity, present a working definition of the concept and then provide perspectives and contexts within which the various facets of ethnic identity are played out. To emphasize the nature of the concept, its opposite, alienation, is also treated. Part II focuses on the functional dynamics of ethnicity and concentrates on three major areas: a) significant forces of assimilation, b) selected models of ethnic identity change, and c) the social and psychological causes and functions of ethnicity. The objective then is to present a compilation of ideas on the anatomy and functional dynamics of ethnicity for both the heuristic purposes of presentation to the student of ethnicity as well as to suggest a theoretical organization of concepts and principles that point to further directions of research.

The decade of the seventies evidenced a great deal of attention given to the ethnic factor in modern society. Such earlier works as Glazer and Moynihan (1963), Gordon (1964), and Schermerhorn (1970) focused upon interethnic relations. Later works such as Greeley (1971, 1974) and Sowell (1978) focused upon the distinctive features of ethnic groups in

America. Those works elaborating the cross-cultural
perspectives on ethnicity such as Cohen (1974),
Henry (1976), Despres (1974) and Glazer and
Moynihan (1975), provided analytical frameworks and
data for the understanding of ethnicity in plural
societies around the world. The ideological essays,
one of the most popular of which is Novak (1972) was
a very important force in popularizing the issue of
ethnicity. However, these are but a few of the
spate of writers and researchers on the subject which
has become a dominant focus for social scientists
in the seventh decade of our century.

The "new ethnicity" movement among academics
essentially generated a shift in our general
understanding of ethnicity. As Glazer and Moynihan
point out about ethnic groups:

> formerly seen as <u>survivals</u> from
> an earlier age, to be treated
> variously with annoyance, toler-
> ation, or mild celebration, we
> now have a growing sense that
> they may be <u>forms</u> of social life
> that are capable of renewing
> and transforming themselves
> (1975, p. 4).

Therefore, in reexamining this phenomenon of ethnicity
we may be exploiting another avenue toward our
understanding of the process of social change and
our adaptive mechanisms and strategies for coping
with and helping to change the present nature of our
modern society.

PART I
THE MAJOR CONCEPTS
AND THE LEVELS OF THEIR OPERATION

CHAPTER 1

CASTING ETHNICITY INTO SOCIAL PERSPECTIVE

The ethnic group is a unit among both larger and smaller social units of society. It may be considered the largest social grouping in which sentiments are evoked and identity formed in the context of a primary group structure and through the vehicles of particular symbols. In noting the variety of social forms or structures of corporate action that are common in both traditional and modern society we can get a better perspective of where ethnicity is situated in terms of scope, complexity, and function.

1.1. Daniel Bell (1975) lists what he considers to be the five "macrosocial units" of society within which corporate membership in the respective units maintains the social system of a population. The first unit is the nation. This is an effective unit with which a people may identify only when we find a great deal of congruence with a single ethnic culture that makes up that nation (p. 153). The second unit is religion. Especially in traditional societies religion is a very important unit, where strong corporate identities are possible within a shared religious context (Ibid., p. 154). Third, possibly the most important unit of group membership is what Bell calls the "communal" unit. At this level we find group sentiments of larger aggregates of people who maintain "primordial ties" involving a consciousness of kind that unites them through key symbols of group identification. We are most familiar with this unit in the form of the ethnic group and ethnic culture. The fourth unit is social class. Being economically based, this unit is defined in terms of material wealth and social status and associated ideology which shapes the structure of production, distribution, and consumption of material goods. The fifth macrosocial unit is sex. Society is divided into males and females and associated sex roles within society (Ibid., pp. 157-158). In traditional societies these units are the contexts of ascribed roles, where the members of a society have little control or influence over their own destiny with regard to their membership in these units. In contemporary times though, under conditions of rapid social change, and with the social mobility and modernization that accompanies this social change, members of these societies find that there is a much greater latitude for conscious and planned choice of group identification and attachment (Ibid., p. 153).

These social units, and those that are discussed below, have within them mechanisms that arouse sentiments, mobilizing and channeling them into thought and behavior appropriate to a particular unit and context. As Bell recognizes, no one unit has dominance in the mobilization of sentiment. An individual's identifications are many and one experiences considerable cross-cutting of group identifications depending on a great many factors both predictable and imponderable. The nature of the cause or adversary, or the type of challenge, threat, or problem that an individual or group encounters can determine which boundary of identification and attachment would become salient, thereby generating a form of political organization and political sentiment (cf. Ibid., p. 157) that would be required to meet a challenge or solve a problem.

1.2. The above typology of macrosocial units of society is only one framework with which to analyze society. A more detailed perspective within which to view the phenomenon of ethnicity is through the social units that the social anthropologist normally uses in the study of human society. These basic social units number seven:

1. The most fundamental of all human ties is the mother-child bond, the psychobiological basis of which generates the deepest of social relationships.

2. The marriage tie, based in the functions of economics and sexuality, is another of the structurally simpler forms of bonding. But, it should be remembered that the monogamous husband-wife bond is only one form of marriage tie, most commonly found in the urban context. (Various forms of polygyny are common in the more traditional cultures).

3. The product of the monogamous marriage bond is the nuclear family which is highly adaptive to the modern urban context. This basic eight role structure (father/husband, mother/wife, son/brother, daughter/ sister) provides the minimal social unit responsible

for the existence and survival of the larger
community as we know it. But, the nuclear family
is only one form of family bonding structure which
is the nucleus of community organization.

4. The extended family is a much more common
form found in the more traditional context outside the
urban industrial complex. It is by no means absent in
the context of modern urban cities, for in the well-
established white ethnic communities and in the Black
communities of urban America the network of extended
kin still functions importantly in maintaining
relative social and economic security. At this point
it may be appropriate to note a form of household
organization that has become well-known in the
literature, found commonly in the Black ghettos of
urban America and also in Caribbean society: the
"matrifocal household." This type of household is
commonly found in areas of poverty where men find
employment unavailable and where women maintain a
household with their children in the absence of
economically-supporting husbands. I prefer to call
this a matrifocal household rather than a matrifocal
family because in many cases this household is couched
in a rather widespread network of extended and
adopted (fictive) kin, including brothers, sisters,
aunts, uncles, cousins, and grandparents as well as
parents, many of whom may live geographically
dispersed from each other yet nevertheless in
communication with each other. The best documentation
for this is found in the anthropological studies of
Black American families.

5. The peer group, based on relative age, is
found universally in human society. Whether in the
context of work, play, education, initiation and
participation in communal associations, or
socialization in general, the peer group is a
mediating structure between the individual and the
socializing senior generations of elders who maintain
the traditional ethnic culture.

6. The village or hamlet is yet another level
of social unit that is composed of members proximal
to each other and very often bound by marriage and
kin ties.

7. The ethnic group is one of the largest
social forms that can maintain social and cultural

4

cohesiveness through space and time. This will be elaborated below.

These seven levels of social unit are most likely to be based on particularistic relationships where personal ties complement a shared cultural experience. Larger, more complex, structures of society based on more universalistic, impersonal, and formalized relations are seen in the contexts of the macrosocial units and larger political institutions such as the town, the city, and the state, which are more directly related to the functions of maintaining the integrity of the larger society as a whole.

CHAPTER 2

THE CONCEPT OF ETHNICITY

In starting out our analysis of the concept of ethnicity we can subsume three analytical levels of systemic operation: The psychological level, the sociological or social structural level, and the cultural level. The psychological level focuses most importantly on the problem of ethnic identity which includes the individual's orientation to his own ethnicity, the sense and extent of one's commitment to the traditions or to the style of life associated with a particular ethnicity, the conflicts that one deals with by maintaining an ethnicity, or the conflicts resolved by one's attachment to their ethnicity, and of course, the general cognitive meaning this ethnicity has for the person. At the sociological level we must consider the social network which defines one's ethnic group. This social network and the frequency of contacts with ethnic familiars tends to define that boundary which associates and identifies one with a particular ethnic group and tradition and social status. It also quite often refers to one's reference group and the rights and duties that bind one into a particular ethnic tradition of that group. At the cultural level we subsume ethnic culture, comprising, on the one hand, the traditions, history, and values that preserve and maintain ideas, sentiments, and codes of social action and individual conduct, and on the other hand, the symbolic content and the contemporary meaning that ethnicity has with regard to the group's present concerns, goals, and problems.

These three levels of ethnicity are characterized as having a gemeinschaft or particular-istic sociocultural perspective that the members share in their ethnic culture. It is a "we-feeling" or communaute de conscience; a social modality of expression most characterized by the primary group orientation. Further, this community consciousness is reinforced and enhanced by a cultural orientation found in just about every human population: ethnocentrism. First conceived by William Graham Sumner, the American sociologist, the concept has become the focus of intensive study (see LeVine and Campbell, 1972). Sumner defined ethnocentrism as follows:

> Ethnocentrism is the technical
> name for this view of things in
> which one's own group is the center
> of everything, and all others are
> scaled and rated with reference to
> it. Folkways correspond to it to
> cover both the inner and the outer
> relation. Each group nourishes its
> own pride and vanity, boasts itself
> superior, exalts its own divinities
> and looks with contempt on outsiders.
> Each group thinks its own folkways
> the only right ones, and if it
> observes that other groups have
> other folkways, these excite its
> scorn. Opprobrious epithets are
> derived from these differences....
> For our present purpose the most
> important fact is that ethnocen-
> trism leads a people to exaggerate
> and intensify everything in their
> own folkways which is peculiar and
> which differentiates them from
> others. It therefore strengthens
> the "folkways" (Sumner, 1906, pp.
> 12-13; as quoted from LeVine and
> Campbell, 1972, p. 8).

The sense of what is good, proper, valued, distinctive;
the feeling of security within a well-defined grouping,
as opposed to the complex pluralism and impersonality
of American society, generates probably one of the
more powerful boundary-maintaining mechanisms for
one's ethnic culture and identity.

CHAPTER 3

THE ETHNIC GROUP

There are many formal definitions of ethnic group that help us to more clearly articulate what the phenomenon actually is; its operational definition, how it is perceived by in-group members and how individuals and groups perceive and define other-than-their-own groups. A more abstract conceptualization has been given by Barth (1969, pp. 9-38) and, more recently, by LeVine and Campbell (1972, p. 105). LeVine and Campbell were interested in working up a formal definition of a social (or ethnic) group, whereas Barth was more interested in identifying ethnic boundary-maintaining mechanisms, those forces and processes that keep ethnic groups identifiable entities. Here, I combine their contributions to provide a working definition of an ethnic group at a relatively abstract level. The first six points are from LeVine and Campbell and the second six are from Barth.

1. There is a high degree of shared distinctive features that are most often ascribed through cultural tradition. There is a considerable amount of common sharing of physical, cultural, social, and psychological attributes among the members of an ethnic group.

2. Members of an ethnic group have a high degree of proximity to each other. That is, persons maintain relatively close distance to each other in space and time, forming communities geographically distinct from the larger urban context, or maintaining networks of contact among members in separate communities.

3. A common history, or historical experience, and a shared destiny can readily maintain patterns of identity amongst the members of an ethnic group.

4. There is a cultural pattern continuity where patterns of behavior remain relatively stable through time and have a good consonance with patterns of thinking and values.

5. A greater intensity of communication exists among the members of an ethnic group than between

8

ethnic groups. Here we find a continuous exchange of ideas and feelings and experience among ethnic members which allows for a gradual process of adaptation to the larger society.

6. Any defined social or ethnic group has boundary-impermeability where a considerable amount of resistance is generated against the intrusion of sociocultural elements from the outside which are considered foreign, unfamiliar, or in some way pose a threat to the integrity of the group.

7. Ascribed status categories of different groups will emphasize the particular status of a given ethnic group. As seen in American society, there is a cultural orientation toward status differences, and a particular ethnic group may have a more or less clear idea of where they stand in this status hierarchy.

8. Demographic balances of different groups in a large population will create population pressures of varying degrees that can intensify identity differences, especially when these pressures generate a competition among the different groups for society's critical resources.

9. Resource competition mobilizes various ethnic populations in their respective quests for scarce but necessary resources that allow for survival at various living standards.

10. Adequate and effective role performance of the ethnic group members is vital in order to make possible the competition for resources. The most critical form of role performance here is political role performance which allows one power to compete successfully for scarce economic resources upon which the group depends.

11. Given the above variables we can also include adequate satisfaction of identity needs that will derive from political effectiveness, economic access, and the freedom to achieve certain desired cultural goals. This, in turn, would facilitate a secure and relatively stable domestic group organization providing a foundation for adequate personality development and a commitment to the ethnic group's ideals, which, in turn, would feed

back upon and nourish one's original identity
thereby satisfying the need.

12. Still very manifest in modern society
today are the variables of political discrimination
and oppression which effectively isolate a group
from the rest of society.

The classical sociologist, Max Weber, who, in
his Economy and Society defined his concept of the
ethnic group, placed emphasis upon mechanisms that
facilitate communal or corporate group action among
people whose aggregate was much larger than any
particular kin group. Weber identified the ethnic
group as one which shared a common descent and
culture among its members and which maintained itself
out of a need for mobilizing larger-than-kin
aggregates from time to time. As quoted in Parsons
and Shils, et.al., 1961, but paraphrased in spots to
smooth out the rough translation:

> Those human groups that entertain
> a subjective belief in their
> common descent because of
> similarities of physical type or
> of customs or because of shared
> memories of colonization and
> migration, where this belief is
> important for the continuation
> of nonkinship communal relation-
> ships, this group shall be called
> ethnic group.... The ethnic group
> differs from the kinship group
> precisely in being a group which
> believes in its common descent
> but yet does not necessarily
> function as a community with
> corporate group action as a
> kinship group might do. In our
> present sense, the ethnic
> community itself is not a
> community; it only facilitates
> communal relationships. It
> facilitates and promotes all
> types of communal relationships,
> particularly in the political
> sphere (vol. I, p. 306).

Weber also suggests that even where ethnic membership

and identity existed as a function of a political community, ethnic membership can still persist long after that political community has ceased to exist because of the personalized ties that have developed. With his notion of the "transmutation of rational associative relationships into personalized communal relationships" (Ibid., p. 306) Weber suggests that it may be a lawful process that transforms relatively long-term impersonal rationalized relationships existing in a particular social network into more personalized social ties with a more salient affective element.

Robert Schermerhorn defines the ethnic group as

> a collectivity within a larger society having real or putative common ancestry, memories of a shared historical past, and a cultural focus on one or more symbolic elements defined as the epitome of their peoplehood (1970, p. 12).

Examples of symbolic elements here would include language or dialect, kinship, religion, physical proximity, nationality, or physical features of the people.

Talcott Parsons sees the ethnic group as a "generic organizational type" characterized as a "diffusely solidary collectivity" (1975, p. 51). It is a "fiduciary" type of association involving a loyalty among the members which binds them into a "moral community" a la Durkheim (Ibid., p. 61). Those factors that act as binding forces and contribute to the maintenance of the ethnic boundaries have been summarized by Isajiw in his survey of twenty-seven definitions used by various social scientists. The following were common attributes of ethnic groups recognized by various social scientists (1974, p. 117).

1. a common national or geographic origin or common ancestors.

2. similar culture or customs

3. shared religion

4. similar race or physical features

5. language

6. consciousness of kind or "we feeling,"
    a sense of loyalty to their peoplehood

7. gemeinschaft relations

8. common values or ethos

9. involvement in a set of institutions
    separate from the larger political society

10. minority status, subordinate status, or
    dominant status

11. ethnic group often cited as an immigrant
    group

Barth's more generalized definition should also be
noted here. He lists four general features of
ethnic groups:

> 1) largely biologically self-
> perpetuating
> 2) shares fundamental cultural
> values, realized in overt unity
> in cultural forms
> 3) makes up a field of communica-
> tion and interaction
> 4) has a membership which identi-
> fies itself, and is identified by
> others, as constituting a category
> distinguishable from other cate-
> gories of the same order (1969
> pp. 10-11).

And lastly, DeVos defines the ethnic group as

> a self-perceived group of people
> who hold in common a set of tra-
> ditions not shared by the others
> with whom they are in contact.
> Such traditions typically include
> "folk" religious beliefs and
> practices, language, a sense of
> historical continuity, and a

common ancestry or place of
origin. The group's actual
history often trails off into
legend or mythology, which
includes some concept of an
unbroken biological-genetic
generational continuity, sometimes regarded as giving special
characteristics to the group.
Endogamy is usual, although
various patterns for intiat-
ing outsiders into the ethnic
group are developed in such a
way that they do not disrupt
the sense of generational
continuity (1975, p. 9).

Within this definition we see the matrix of what
Geertz (1963) after Shils, (1957) calls "primordial
sentiments:" those feelings and attachments to
ascribed features of one's physical, psychological,
and social environments, such as region of origin,
religion and language, and kinship and genealogy all
of which comprise the referents of an individual's
and a group's identity; the feeling of belonging and
the belief in having an important role to play in the
carrying out of the group's shared destiny.

CHAPTER 4

ETHNIC CULTURE

Ethnic culture can be conceived of as a subset of culture in general. In fact, to a great extent, the difference is only a matter of scale where a smaller distinctive culture exists within a larger encompassing culture. I define the concept of culture as follows:

> Culture is a system of symbols, widely shared in a population, learned through and dependent upon language, the communication of which occurs in a social context and is established as convention and tradition, functioning as an orientational framework for behavior, thought, and feeling.

This is a complex definition that must be elaborated. By symbols, I refer to those material and non-material artifacts of communication that refer to other things beyond their own intrinsic significance. Such things as cuisine, home furnishings, religious artifacts like statues, pictures, and crosses are examples of material symbols whereas the mother-tongue, ethnic music, the meaning of authority figures, and history may be examples of the non-material symbols. These symbols act as vehicles of conception, cueing off particular kinds of sentiment, beliefs, and values that go far beyond the immediate meaning and function of the symbolic object itself. By system, I refer to a high degree of relatedness between the symbols which are grouped into smaller and larger configurations. For example, a particular ethnic culture may conceive of the father/husband as the stern but just patriarch and of the mother/wife as a submissive but strong and giving "Madonna" figure associated with concepts and symbols of honor, dominance and submission, filial piety, and so forth. And, in another segment of the ethnic culture, the religious sphere, we most likely will find beliefs and codes that complement and reinforce the structure of the family. These symbolic configurations may be grouped into the categories of kinship, economics, political organization, religion, etc., i.e., those institutions that make up the ethnic community as a whole.

Symbol systems, though, are highly dependent upon language, for without language among human beings, very little communication takes place. However, human language encompasses more than speech and grammar. There is also a great and largely unexplored realm of nonverbal communication. The language of the body, kinesics, communicates through gesture, posture, and muscle tension or flaccidity. The language of space relations, proxemics, communicates through relative distances that people keep from one-another. And then there is paralanguage, the spacing and stressing of words as well as their intonation. Language, in all its forms and nuances, structures and conditions our thinking, our perception of sensation, and our emotions. One has only to observe communication patterns among the Italians compared to WASPS, Arabs compared to English or French, or Jews compared to Black Americans to understand that distinctive configurations of communication exist among members of different ethnic cultures.

Convention and tradition are two integrally related components of culture. By convention we are referring to a widespread agreement about customs, conduct, beliefs, and general assumptions about the world held by a particular population. The term also involves a social component that people largely carry out their customs in a social context. In most cases the population holds to these customs with considerable resistance to change, which is understandable in the light of the fact that much of culture consists of adaptive strategies that have been learned through trial and error with a great deal of expense of human energy; a myriad of solutions to everyday problems which make living more predictable and secure. The concept of tradition refers to the transgenerational perspective of convention; knowledge, customs, beliefs, in a word, conventions, passed down from one generation to the next, developing a feeling of security and strength through a sense of history and generating a repository of cultural resources from which to draw enrichment and adaptability. In contradistinction to this perspective, however, we must also realize that in modern society, and in a highly technologized culture, many traditions lose their function, their usefulness, and new adaptive strategies and cultural resources must be invented to solve problems traditions were not capable of dealing with.

Orientational framework refers to the way a person or a group relates to the world and the meaning that that world has for them. It directs or shapes the inclination to behave in a certain way. What can be said of an orientational framework in particular can be said about a culture in general. This concept encompasses a whole "family" of other concepts that point out its complexity (cf Hughes, 1976,p. 73), such as assumptions about the world and more specific meanings built up out of these assumptions that provide the basis for explanations and understandings. The orientational framework operates with configurations of ideas and images associated with certain feelings or attitudes that have their focus on someone or some thing. They are usually the basis for certain values which guide behavior and social action. Orientational framework most importantly involves rules and sets of rules known better as codes which are the basis for standards and ideals of personal conduct and social action, better known as social norms.

Culture in general, and ethnic culture in particular, functions in at least four general modalities. First, culture is adaptive. Through trial and error, learning and experimentation, through play and diligence and perseverance, human beings generate ideas about the world, methodologies by which to survive and grow, and social patterns that integrate human groups with their environment, wherever they live. Second, culture is pragmatic. Human beings are very pragmatic animals, much of the time. The idea, belief, or method that works is valued. That which appears to accomplish the goal and reward the person and group in that accomplishment becomes part of the cultural inventory. This also emphasizes a situational priority over an ideal or norm. One may have to compromise an ideal in order to gain a more immediate need; it is the practical and the utilitarian concerns that shape a group's orientation as well as those more distant or abstract ideals toward which more people strive than reach. Third, culture is expressive. Humans must express inner needs and demonstrate feelings, attitudes, orientations, and beliefs. The expressive modality of culture is manifest through religion, the arts such as dance, drama, poetry, sculpture, painting, and even the culinary arts.

Individual expressivity is demonstrated everyday and group expressivity is seen on especially designated days of ceremonial festivity and ritual. Fourth, culture is explanatory. Through language, beliefs, ideology, philosophy, and religion, explanations are provided; explanations that offer a foundation of meaning and understanding that creates a perspective through which one relates to the world.

CHAPTER 5

ETHNIC IDENTITY

When we speak of a person's identity we are referring to aspects of the world that one has taken over as their own, both consciously and unconsciously; the energy and commitment to persons and groups, ideas and ideals; perseverance toward reaching goals that results in building one's personality; individuals that one has modelled one's self after, and more importantly, the social roles that one has adapted to, and in some cases, created for one's self. To be more precise, it is the symbolic meaning of these aspects of the world that one takes over as part of the self that is of importance here. To refer to a person's "identity" though is something of a generalization, technically, because, in fact, a personality consists of many "identities" (internalized components of the world) that function together to make up a whole and viable individual. And, of course, these aspects of the world are not taken over or adopted in their original wholeness or entirety, but rather, an individual, usually unconsciously, selects aspects of a component that are meaningful, aspects of someone or something that can become integrated with the rest of the existing personality. And, to be realistic, we must also recognize that individuals internalize many things that do not integrate well with other aspects of their personality, and this results in greater or lesser personality or identity conflicts. These identities are built up over time through childhood maturational and socialization processes and continue to a lesser extent into adulthood.

In examining the concept of ethnic identity we should recognize at least four different perspectives: 1) the social scale or various social fields an individual interacts in; 2) the distinction between cultural ethnic identity and social ethnic identity; 3) the perspective of time; and 4) the problem of alienation. With regard to social scale we note at least three different levels of social field out of which identity formation takes place: First is the field of the primary group made up of one's closest kin, most importantly one's mother and father or parent surrogates much of whose behavior, attitudes and emotional responses the child takes over as one's own. Second is the field of the extended kin or relatives outside one's nuclear family who may have some influence on the developing individual. Especially in well-established and conservative ethnic groups, the three generation extended kin group is most important in preserving the ethnic tradition. The third social field is the category of secondary groups, church, school, voluntary associations, whose ideals and goals one ascribes to and takes over as one's own in order to emulate them and become to some extent like them, enabling one to take on desired social roles and status in the community. Important as these fields are in the formation of identity in general and ethnic identity in particular, another very important component of identity should not be forgotten, and that is the distinctive, induplicable, psychobiological self that is delivered from the womb of one's mother and is the matrix from which, the foundation upon which, an individual's and a group's identity is established.

The perspective of social vs. cultural ethnic identity becomes particularly important in contexts of modern urban change because there could be a perceivable difference between the social network one is involved in and the values and symbols, history and beliefs, that one espouses. In the process of societal change and assimilation there are four logical possibilities: First, a person may be moving up the social ladder and appear to be assimilating in order to maximize the rewards of the greater society. Therefore, we will see the networks of social relationships be, most likely, non-ethnic. Yet, in the seclusion of the domestic group, and in the background of one's day-to-day activities, the ethnic culture, the beliefs, values, and orientations, may still be dominant. Or, one may maintain endogamous social networks within the ethnic group, but be developing more assimilated ideas, values, and beliefs more characteristic of the wider American society. Or, one may have become almost completely assimilated and espouse very little, if any, of the ethnic culture, and have only minimal relationships with those of his ethnic group. Or, one may have neither given up the ethnic culture nor separated himself from the network of ethnic ties, and therefore, will have maintained the tradition of ethnicity to a great extent.

From the perspective of time, we may see how ethnic identity may function in different temporal realms. Traditional ethnic identity has a predominantly past time orientation. It is "embedded in the cultural heritage... of the group" (DeVos and Romanucci-Ross, p. 364). That aspect of one's ethnic identity consists of those elements that are part of one's ethnic culture including the history, customs, cuisine, and art forms; those things that a particular individual embraces, takes over as part of one's self, and uses to further that ethnic heritage. Most of our social roles and identity tied up in these roles occur in the present time orientation. Although ethnicity related activities are acted out in the present with daily cuisine (if ethnic foods are consumed on a daily or regular basis), use of an ethnic language, and the like, it is usually the non-ethnic type of activities and social roles that are predominant in the present orientation of daily life. Those aspects of life relevant in this context include one's profession or job or daily mode of making a living that is not attached to a legitimate occupation role, fraternal orders, social class, activities attached to the housewife/mother role, the role of the student, and so forth. The time orientation to the future involves identities attached to roles that are primarily oriented to situations, ideals, and states of affairs that have not yet been attained. Relevant here are social and religious movements that are striving toward changing and raising the standards and life conditions on one's group or class. In many cases the factor of ethnicity has played a very important part: to wit, the Black Muslim, Panther, and Civil Rights movements; the American Indian Movement, and the extensive Chicano efforts. In these cases we would probably see the strongest identities among those who were the leaders and the disciples of the particular groups while those with the weaker identities would be those who had yet to make a full or total commitment to their movement.

The problem of alienation involves the loss of identity with a person, role, or symbol. Probably the process most responsible for the dissipation of ethnic identity is assimilation. The problem of, and research on, assimilation and alienation is complex and far-reaching and has been treated well by sociologists and social psychologists and cannot be elaborated here. Suffice it to say that assimilation and alienation are processes that oppose, conflict with, and take away ethnic identification. Assimilation is usually seen as a unidirectional process where an individual goes from a comparatively restricted identity with the extended kin and ethnic group to a widely diffused identification with various social roles and American cultural symbols, which may also include a narrower identity structure as is found among professionals. The process of alienation is not unidirectional since one may at one time become alienated from his ethnic group and its symbols as he assimilates into the wider American fabric of social life, and then at another time become alienated from much of the non-ethnic and secular American culture only to readopt aspects of one's ethnic heritage or adopt some other more restricted form of identity such as becoming a member of a professional group or getting involved with a social or religious movement. In any case, the problem of alienation, the phenomenon whereby a person gives up the commitments, the attachments, the symbols that, at least in part, helped define the self, is a very important problem to recognize if the dynamics of ethnic identity is to be properly understood.

Changes in an individual's interests and changes in the adaptive strategies for living in the world will likely attenuate or eradicate old identities while new ones are built up. But, in this regard, especially when considering ethnic identity, we must also remember that vestiges of old identities do remain within the personality structure of the individual. It is especially important to realize that those who have so earnestly strived to shed their old ethnic identities in their quest to become fully "American" may have done so at the price of repressing social identity needs that contributed to their original sense of security, or, have seen their alienated ethnicity reappear in the interests and activities of their adolescent and adult children. In many cases today, that "subjective sense of continuity in belonging" (DeVos, p. 16) is being revived in what many have called the "new ethnicity."

21

As Durkheim said in his classic <u>Elementary Forms of Religious Life</u>, man achieves a sense of self, at least partially, out of his sense of belonging to a group.

PART II

THE FUNCTIONAL DYNAMICS OF ETHNICITY

CHAPTER 6

SOME SIGNIFICANT FORCES OF ASSIMILATION

Although America, from the beginning, has been a nation of relatively rapid change, by the turn of the century the society of Americans was fairly well-established. The institutional macrostructure and the general cultural orientations provided a matrix from which the national character features of individual personalities would be expressed for several generations to come. The immigrants to the urban regions of America, then, were all subjected to similar forces that generated a common assimilation process. Schermerhorn (1949), in his discussion of the Polish American, cites ten forces that strongly determined the assimilation process. I think these forces are applicable to all ethnic groups who have immigrated to the urban centers of America.

1. A universalistic cultural orientation emphasizes impersonal modes of social relationships, bureaucratic structures, assembly line technology, and a general orientation to role and function rather than personal qualities of the individual performing the service or with whom one is trading. This is in contrast to the particularistic orientation which emphasizes personal relationships, ties of inter-dependency, a greater emotional component, and the salience placed on identification with the person rather than the role.

2. A non- or anti-ethnic sentiment outside the ethnic community generates a pressure, if not a coercion, to become like other Americans in order for ethnics to gain access to some of the society's rewards through the acceptance by significant others.

3. American legal standards were never as rigid and as binding as many parochial codes ensconced in traditional religion such as Roman Catholicism. Liberal legal standards had the effect, at least in part, of loosening marital and family solidarity and allowing for the greater expression of personal goals as opposed to familial duty.

24

4. American individualism is the antithesis of ethnic traditionalism. The ideology and ethos (ideas and values) of American individualism put the greatest emphasis on the priority of satisfying personal needs and attaining individualized goals. This orientation was crucial regarding the problem of human adaptation in the new world. It was not difficult for the sons of the immigrants to see that the old ways yielded little in the way of solutions to new problems, yielded little in the way of path-finding through the complexities of the American social structure. Rather, it was the creativity and the aggressiveness of the newcomer and the following generation that was needed to establish a community and to achieve an integration into the new society.

5. Opportunities for social mobility presented themselves for those who took the initiative and who had the intelligence and the luck to mount and climb the American social ladder to success. To most it was not hard to see that the direction of the climb led away from tradition, familial networks, and old world values.

6. America's occupational diversity led members of a family into different walks of life, and this had the consequence of dividing the interests of family members as well as limiting the plane of common experience from which familial members could identify and relate to one-another.

7. The degree of sexual emancipation in America was a worry, if not startling, to immigrants who maintained orthodox controls over their growing and maturing children. The absence of the require-ment of a chaperone on a date itself had the consequence of putting a large part of the responsibility on the shoulders of the teenagers or young adults, who, in their own ways, were becoming more and more predisposed to following their own routes to intimacy.

8. Public schools, of course, are a major formal institutionalized mode for transmitting American macroculture to the neophyte children in their most impressionable years. This was commonly known among the members of most, if not all, ethnic groups, and where ethnic parents found this mode of

education unacceptable, an alternative course of resistance was taken with the establishment of parochial schools sponsored through Church efforts.

9. The novelty of city life appeared very attractive to the children and young adults of immigrant parents. The lure of new experience, the city glitter, movies and other modes of mass communication, heterogeneity of people mixing together in business and fun drew the young ethnics out of their ghettos and pointed them in directions that contradicted many traditions of the old ethnic culture.

10. The formation and establishment of nuclear families is a typical if not necessary adaptation to modern industrial urban life. The nuclear family emerged as an independent economic unit that attentuated a great deal of influence that the traditional extended family had on its members. Probably one of the most significant consequences of the establishment of the nuclear family was the breaking away from the traditional rules of endogamy which defined the boundaries within which ethnic members could engage in social relations. Rules which required that a person marry another only from one's own ethnic group and religion was the most important requirement involved in an ethnic group's rules of endogamy. The nuclear family and its greater independence from the traditional hold of the three generation extended family allowed for violations of these rules of endogamy to a greater and greater extent from one generation to the next.

The systematic functional interrelations between these and other forces created a synergistic effect that determined the direction of change in ethnic culture and identity. However, the currents of ethnic cultures still run rather strongly through American culture giving the latter no small part of its national cultural identity. The "Why?" of the contemporary viability of American ethnic cultures and identities lies in the problem of determining the causes and functions of contemporary ethnicity, discussed in chapter 8.

CHAPTER 7

MODELS OF ETHNIC IDENTITY CHANGE

The process of ethnic identity change has not
been very thoroughly explored, yet several models of
ethnic identity dynamics have suggested the nature
and direction of change through several stages.

7.1. As early as 1937, the historian Marcus
Lee Hansen stated (what I believe is a Jewish proverb),
"What the son wishes to forget, the grandson wishes
to remember" (1937:15). From his study he derived
what is known as Hansen's Law which holds that the
immigrant generations maintain a well-marked pluralism,
segregating themselves from the potentially hostile
elements of the host society, while the first generation born in the U.S. (Hansen and many sociologists
call this the second generation) is marked by the
characteristic of assimilation, whereby that generation makes a considerable attempt to throw off its
immigrant identity and status which is felt to be a
stigma. However, the second generation born in the
U.S. is said to experience an identity crisis and
feels very ill at ease at being just an American.
The heterogeneity of America does not provide an
adequate structure for a stable or secure identity,
so this generation goes back to a form of pluralism
whereby ethnic boundaries are reinstated and ethnic
identities are reestablished. Although this model
was rather crude and relatively weak in supporting
data, it nevertheless initiated the attempt to understand the nature and direction of change in American
ethnic identity.

7.2. A more detailed model of the assimilation
process and identity change is given by Daniel Glaser
in his "Dynamics of Ethnic Identification" (1958).
Although this model is laid out as a series of stages,
it is meant to be conceived of as a continuum where
one stage gradually merges with the next in accordance
with complex psychosocial intermediating processes.

The first stage in this model is called the
segregating stage. This refers to the immigrant
generation which may segregate itself in the new
American community and look to each other for social
and emotional support and identity. The individuals

27

appear to be highly ethnocentric in their thinking and feel markedly distinct from the rest of society. In its extremes individuals may become paranoid about the dominant members and attempt to insulate themselves as much as possible against the possible dangers of the outside. Segregating indivuals often strive toward maintaining their ethnic identity as an end in itself even in the face of deleterious consequences of this.

The second stage is called marginal. This stage is marked by uncertainty in the individual. The ethnic person has been subjected to a certain amount of assimilation and is inconsistently relating to out-group members, sometimes in a positive way, other times negatively. And, on the other hand, out-group members may be accepting at one time and rejecting at other times. The ethnic member may be segregating in the context of his own group, but when in the company of out-group members may exhibit behavior more acceptable to those members. As a marginal person he has some anxiety about his social identity and therefore is other-directed, letting others determine what he will say and how he will behave.

The third stage in this continuum is the desegregating stage. In this stage the ethnic person seeks to avoid any and all associations with his ethnic group in his quest for assimilation and acceptance by the larger society. In his eagerness to adopt a new identity, and thereby reap the greater rewards of society, he may become highly critical of the ascribed ethnic group from which he emerged. This stage is often characterized by self-hate and the members involved in this stage often adopt the stereotypes and prejudices toward one's own ethnic group that are held by the out-group members. The person's assimilation has progressed to the point where much less discrimination is experienced and, with some effort, the minority group member can establish himself in the larger society without the stigma afforded those still identified with the original ethnic group. This person seeks the approval of members of the dominant group and thinks in ways consonant with the dominant American ideology while at the same time alienating those members of his ascribed ethnic group that could jeopardize his newfound status as an assimilated American.

The fourth and last stage is that of assimilation. Glaser realizes that this represents a logical extension of his model, but does not necessarily represent a significant segment of a population since most individuals, and certainly all groups, fall short of this ideal-typical limit. When one is totally assimilated one does not categorize others according to ascribed features of ethnicity but normally is oriented toward the acceptance of others on the basis of individual qualities. Instead of the usual ethnocentric orientation toward other groups, the assimilated individual's orientation is one of cultural relativity. Ideally, the assimilated individual integrates elements from many realms of his society and culture into a more or less stable personal identity.

A postulate of this stage model is that the stages cannot be skipped. Each stage is a logical and necessary precondition for the next and a logical and necessary consequence of the preceding stage. A second postulate is that one can go backwards as well as forwards along this stage continuum. There are well documented studies today that point out previously well assimilated individuals turning back to a more parochial way of life, either based on one's former ethnicity, or adopting a new ethnicity with which to identify.

Associated with these stages are descriptive qualities that differentiate one stage from another. These qualities are divided into three categories: ideology, association preferences (the type of people one wishes to associate with), and emotionality (the feelings associated with one's ethnic group). The diagram below notes the qualities under each category associated with each respective stage. A third postulate of this model is that in arriving at a particular stage in identity change one might get there either by first adopting the ideology of the stage then developing the associations, and then coming to have the attendant feelings about the stage. Or, one might work in the reverse, first having certain feelings, developing the associations with the desired others, and then learning and adopting the ideology. The former direction is called in

Stage-Markers	Ethnic Ideology	Associated Preferences in-group members	Emotionality
segregating	ethnocentrism		solidarity, security, xenophobia
marginal	in-group ideology but ambivalent valuation	inconsistent, some out-group associations	considerable anxiety, fear of rejection
desegregating	low valuation of ascribed identity, assimilation ideology	alienates in-group (other-directed)	disgust, self-hate of in-group identity, conforms to dominant group
assimilated	American egalitarian	no ethnic preferences	acceptance on basis of individual qualities

-------ideological conversion------>

<------reflexive conversion-------

Glaser's terms, ideological conversion and the reverse is called reflexive conversion.

Glaser's model can be applicable to whole ethnic groups, to generations, or to individuals by themselves. Through the use of statistical strategies it may be possible to classify whole ethnic groups as to where they are modally positioned on this continuum. In other words, in a statistical sample, if the majority or significant segment of the group fell into the desegregating class, that group could be said to be modally desegregating, with a certain range of variation and a standard deviation around the mode. Or, one may find it possible to use a generational generalization where we might say that the immigrant generation was segregating, the first generation born in America was marginal, the second generation was desegregating, and so on. Or, one may find that individuals by themselves either stay at a particular stage all their lives, or at the other extreme, travel through the whole range of stages within a specific period of their lifetimes.

7.3. Our last model of ethnic identity change and assimilation is a six phase process offered to us by Andrew Greeley (1971, chapter 4). The first phase is the immigrant's experience upon entering the United States. It is the phase called "cultural shock." It is characterized by disorientation, fear, disorganization; where the immigrant is met with greater or lesser hostility by the already-established members of American society; where the main issue for the immigrant is "sheer survival."

Phase two is called "organization and emerging self-consciousness." Here we find leadership emerging among the various ethnic enclaves from such realms as the clergy, the political precinct, fraternal organizations, and in journalism. In this phase we find the immigrants learning the English language while their children are (largely) in public school. There is upward occupational and social mobility: from unskilled to skilled workers, from student to professional, from relative poverty to the accumulation of wealth, and from political impotence to political power.

Phase three involves the "assimilation of the

elite." Normally it is the leaders of a community who begin the assimilation first since they are the ones instrumental in adapting themselves and their groups to the new culture and social environment. In this phase we find the struggle to win acceptance. With the assistance of the leaders of an ethnic group much of that group climbs to the lower middle class. Some break out of the "ethnic mobility pyramids" and merge into the mainstream of American life, but this usually necessitates shunning their "ignoble" ethnic backgrounds in order to win that greater acceptance needed to become successful in the wider American community.

Phase four Greeley calls the phase of "militancy." Here we find the ethnic group emerging as fully middle class, with some members already solidly in the upper middle class. The organized ethnic community now attempts to develop and maintain their own cultural and social institutions modelled after those in the wider society. The militancy Greeley refers to is the zeal and the attempt to outdo American institutions with similar functions. And so we have the ethnic arts associations, drama and dance groups; we also note the debutant's ball, elaborate confirmations, bar mitzvahs, and not-to-be-outdone weddings. And there are beneficient associations, financial cooperatives and credit unions. Greeley specifically cites the institution of American Catholicism which built up agencies and institutions separate from the WASP society in many professional and social service areas that were primarily patronized by members of specific ethnic communities. With the organized ethnic community exploiting its newly-won power it easily comes into conflict with other groups vying for similar resources.

Phase five: "self-hatred and antimilitancy." The more accepted and assimilated new generation is now embarrassed by the strident and abrasive thrusts of the militant people and groups of their respective ethnic communities. These newer elites are now alienating themselves from their ethnicity so as to become more acceptable to the macrosociety and because they are in more agreement with the ideals and values of the wider American culture. These

people become very critical of their own group's
ethnic culture and tradition. There is a great
push for social change and "modernization" and at the
same time there are vestiges of irresistible ties
to the ethnic culture that create conflicts yet to
be resolved.

Phase six is the phase of "emerging adjustment."
As Greeley reminds us of Hansen's dictum, "What the
father forgets the son remembers," we see the new
generation bringing no zealous pride, yet no shame
about its ethnic heritage. The new generation is
curious about its history and willing to retrace its
roots back to lost traditions and ideas, yet remain
ensconced in the mainstream of American life.

7.4. The more recent research on language
use and the communication of ethnicity by Vladimir
Nahirny and Joshua Fishman generally supports these
models of ethnic identity change. Their specific
ideas are important enough to consider here in some
detail. The central thesis is that

> the erosion of ethnicity and ethnic
> identity experienced by most (but
> not all) American ethnic groups
> takes place in the course of three
> generations; it involves, in other
> words, the immigrant fathers, their
> sons and their grandsons. Contrary
> to the widely prevalent opinion
> that there ensues some kind of a
> return to the fold of ethnicity,
> whenever any immigrant group
> reaches the third generation stage
> of its development, we hold that
> the ethnic heritage, including the
> ethnic mother tongue, usually ceases
> to play any viable role in the life
> of the third generation (1965, p.
> 311).

Two points should be brought out regarding this
thesis: First, except for Hansen and Nahirny and
Fishman, the stage models used here do not use
generations as markers. Nahirny and Fishman use
generations as markers and therefore do not

necessarily dispute the fact that there may be more
than three stages in the total process. Second, in
asserting that there is no return to the fold of
ethnicity, the authors are referring to an original
ethnic experience. I don't believe that the authors
are denying the recrudescense of ethnicity or interest
in ethnicity, especially throughout the late 1960's
and early 1970's, but rather, may agree with my point
that the meaning of ethnicity has changed; that the
ethnic interest or ethnic experience of third and
fourth generation individuals who have "gone back"
is quite different from the ethnic experience of their
grandfathers. The ethnic experience of the immigrants, whose life and culture was so different from
what they encountered in their new homeland, could
hardly have been able to effectively communicate it
to a new generation no matter how earnestly they
tried to do so through their inculcation of traditional values and customs to their children.

> Being an outgrowth of past personal
> experience, the ethnic identification
> of the immigrant fathers constituted
> something deeply subjective and
> concrete; that is to say, it was
> hardly externalized or expressed
> in generally symbolic terms
> (p. 314).

> On the whole, this way of life was
> steeped in intimacy and immediacy
> to such an extent that both the
> human and nonhuman worlds within
> it were highly individualized and
> scarcely transferable (p. 313).

The language of the homeland itself housed the
conceptual structures and ways of thinking and feeling that provided the matrix of expression and
experience of ethnicity. A new generation speaking
a different language could hardly share this same
intimate and personal experience. Besides, it was
not until ethnic groups were established in American
society, when ethnic group interaction with other
groups generated conflicts, competition, and the
sensitive awareness of inscrutable differences, did
the general national categories of ethnicity become
established. In the homeland, these people made

cultural distinctions in terms of their village and the region of their country, occupation, and social class, and were relatively insensitive to identity in terms of national political boundaries. As Glazer put it:

> The urbanization of many East Euro-
> pean peoples occurred in America,
> not in Europe, and the effects of
> urbanization, its breaking down of
> local variation, its creation of
> some common denominator of nation-
> ality, its replacement of the sub-
> ideological feelings of villagers
> with a variety of modern ideologies,
> these effects, all significant in
> making the East European peoples
> nations, were in large measure
> first displayed among them here in
> America (Glazer, 1954, p. 166,
> quoted by Greeley, 1971, p. 28).

In America these personal experiences and old identifications were maintained through the establishment of voluntary organizations of many types, such as economic cooperatives, dance and drama groups, and taverns which functioned as local social centers. The need for establishing these organizations must have been very strong. As Nahirny and Fishman state, many of these organizations were established through "sheer human sentiment" (Ibid., p. 315) not only to maintain a common framework for the expression of the old ethnic experience, but also for the insurance of maintaining a sense of predictability and security in a not-too-hospitable society. These organizations, made up of individuals who shared, more or less, local histories, coming from the same village or region, served to maintain localized experiences of their ethnicity, and not, rather, to establish a sense of national identity. The sense of national identity was never very strong, if existent at all, among the immigrant population.

The sons, who comprised the first generation, had new and pressing needs. The culture they met held out rewards and opportunities that were achievable not through the maintenance of their fathers' traditions and experience, but through the

35

enculturation of typically American values and orientations. But, being a product of early socialization by immigrant parents while at the same time being enculturated into a different world of experience the sons faced a conflict. As in the words of the authors:

> ...the attitude of many sons verged on outright nihilism; that is, they tended to dismiss their respective ethnic heritages in toto, either by equating them with ignorance and superstition, or by equating them with poverty and backwardness....
> To appreciate the tragic predicament in which some of the sons found themselves, it suffices to point out that the more intensely they despised their ethnic heritage the more conscious they were of their ethnic identity. The more ashamed they were of this past, and even of their parents, the more they were aware of their ethnic background. For it should be kept in mind that by suppressing ethnicity the sons also rebelled against parts of themselves (p.318).

This conflict had the general tendency to be resolved by dichotomizing the problem, and thereby attenuating the deeper levels of ambivalence. It appears that the more effort that was made to divest one's self of the father's ethnic legacy the more attention was given to the more transcendent values and general codes that were inherent in the old ethnicity, yet not directly acted out or articulated by the ethnic fathers. In this way the sons could maintain some sense of continuity with the parental legacy in "abstracto" while still abnegating the values and traditions of the old ethnicity in "concreto" (p. 322)

> While estranged from the parental heritage, the sons, nevertheless remained more conscious of their ethnic identity than were their immigrant fathers. For the ethnic identity of the fathers was so much

> taken for granted and accepted
> implicitly that they were scarcely
> explicitly conscious of it. On
> the other hand, the marginality
> of the sons made them acutely
> self-conscious and also highly
> sensitive to it; especially when
> passing through adolescence (p. 322).

By the time most sons passed through their adolescence the rift between tradition and modernity was quite well fixed because of generational discontinuity and the formation of two linguistic subgroups within the household.

By the time of the grandsons' generation the mother tongue had become just another foreign language and the traditional ethnic identity posed no threat to the more or less solidified American identity of these grandsons:

> ...in contrast to the sons, the
> grandsons had never experienced
> the full brunt of marginality.
> The grandsons neither sought
> to disavow nor rushed to embrace
> their ethnic past. Increasingly
> it came to approximate an object
> of cognitive orientation, some-
> thing that the grandsons had to
> study in order to acquire
> 'knowledge about' it and in order
> to 'appreciate' it. But such
> knowledge and appreciation is
> usually kept within reasonable
> bounds and need have little or no
> relevance to daily life from the
> selection of spouses to personal
> and organization associations
> (p. 323).

7.5. While these models of ethnic identity change conceive the last or latest stage of change as a predominant tendency toward normalcy, assimilation, or integrative resolution, Stein and Hill have published a study (1971) that focuses on a more pathological direction which is strongly evidenced among certain members of white ethnic groups in the

U.S. This theory will be more fully elaborated in chapter 8, but here I would like to briefly outline the general pattern of change in terms of some of the psychoanalytic concepts that Stein and Hill use in the development of their argument. Although they do not divide the dynamics of change into separate (numbered) stages, for heuristic purposes I shall consider their model as a four stage process.

Stein and Hill consider the white ethnic youth of the third or fourth generation in the 1960's in a state of uneasy assimilated adjustment. In this respect, there is a good deal of agreement with Nahirny and Fishman on the matter of the transmission of ethnic culture from the earlier generation to the more recent generation. (If we are to keep a proper time perspective in using Nahirny and Fishman as a point of departure, we should remember that who Stein and Hill refer to as the "father" is the "son" in the Nahirny and Fishman study; the "son" in the former study is the "grandson" in the latter study). In this stage of uneasy assimilated adjustment, the father has strived to escape the immigrant ethnic stigma of his father and has been moderately successful in his working class level of social and economic mobility. The sons have had little or no ethnic inculcation (this would refer to the "grandsons" in the Nahirny and Fishman study). The son then grows up "Americanized" yet still carrying the subtle or covert ethnic orientations, parochial values and attitudes that become expressed in ways not readily recognizable by the actors themselves. According to Stein and Hill, there has been an active abandonment of ethnic culture on the part of the father and carried on in the generation of the son. This alienation of ethnicity is tied to an alienation of aspects of the father's personality (the son's father as well as the father's father), a form of rejection that has generated a process involving repressed guilt over the disassociation of one's self from what had been cherished in the past. This guilt, which has remained totally at the unconscious level of psychodynamics, is kept at bay and easily managed because of the quest for higher goals of economic and social advancement.

We can consider the second stage to be the period of crisis of the 1960's: The Vietnam War problem, campus dissent and riots, racial flare-ups,

the assassinations of national leaders, the psychedelic
drug and sex oriented counterculture movement in contrast to the rather parochial Catholic ethnic working
class population who viewed the liberationist activities with disgust, rage, and envy. In this period
arose a sense of unfulfilled ambition, increased frus-
tration and shattered dreams among many members of the
white ethnic population who also felt a growing sense
of relative deprivation together with the sense
(imagined or real) of downward social mobility as the
national economy slackened. This experience then
revived or intensified their sense of inferiority,
impotence, and self-hate which had been an experience
of an earlier generation. This experience of self-
abnegation was mostly generated by the white ethnic's
sense of not really having "arrived" in the American
mainstream; they still saw themselves as outsiders,
communities of persons who never realized the attain-
ment of the American Dream of genuine success and full
acceptance by the dominant WASP groups in American
society.

The third stage can be considered a "narcissistic
paranoid regressive reaction" in the words of Stein
and Hill. Finding no realistic direction to further
economic and social advancement, coupled with ever-
heightening frustrations, a specific reaction is
experienced among a large enough number of the white
ethnic population to become expressed at the sociocultural level as the White Ethnic Movement. As the
authors have put it, "boundless rage" had been un-
leashed from the failure of the American Dream.
Anticipatory socialization is abandoned, where the
dominant WASP group is no longer the reference group,
where WASP customs and values are no longer idealized.
This process is regressive in that "dedifferentiation"
occurs (rather than growth through the increasing
differentiation of the personality), romanticization
becomes salient (idealizing certain aspects of life
while devaluing others in a way that does not relate
accurately to reality), and magical thinking becomes a
predominant mode of thought (replacing actual relationships with the ideology of relationships). The process
is narcissistic in that egoistic needs are predominant
over social group needs, where a precarious identity
is shorn up through delusions of superiority, racial
hatred, and flight into the security of an exclusive

group. The process is paranoid in that certain
selected ethnic traits are idealized and considered
unassailably good while other traits of themselves
and their ethnicity are repudiated and projected
onto out-groups, Jews, Blacks, and Latins, which then
easily become the targets of hatred and rationalized
aggression. This divestment of one's own undesirable
characteristics helps greatly in resolving the
ambivalence that is so painful during this period
and assists members of this population in developing
their ethnophilic movement. The process of fixation
and identity foreclosure (which precludes further
psychological growth) is a consequence of this movement whereby fixation and identity foreclosure become
perduring features of the personalities of the members
of this movement. In the fourth stage the movement
continues with its characteristics of ethnic
idealization and separation from the other sociocultural groups through ethnocentric exclusivity,
where a precarious ego is attempted to be strengthened
through mass group identity. This type of movement,
like other nativistic movements around the world,
can be considered a culturally constituted system of
ego defense which prevents further sociocultural
integration and a climate of acceptance of difference;
it precludes a flexibility so vital for adaptation to
sociocultural change.

CHAPTER 8

SOCIAL AND PSYCHOLOGICAL CAUSES AND FUNCTIONS OF ETHNICITY

This section explores further the psychosocial causal-functional variables that appear to play an important role in determining the structure of ethnicity and endowing it with motivational impetus. In this context the discussion will treat the origins of pluralism, political functions, affective bases, the importance of boundaries, and the psychosocial consequences of ethnicity as a social movement.

8.1. The problem of ethnicity gains its salience within the context of urban pluralism. M.G. Smith defines pluralism as the "differential incorporation of social aggregates into a common political society"(1969, p. 430). Glazer and Moynihan suggest that the primary causes of the pluralistic society in the modern world is "the result of more or less sharply defined and not infrequently organized movements of people from one part of the world to another to meet new, and, again, often organized demands for labor" (1975, p. 13). The demand for labor was easily seen by the new groups as the most accessible avenue for gaining the resources and the status rewards that their new homeland extended, if not promised, to them. But, gaining jobs was not an easy task once the population began to swell and many groups vied for labor that was on the way to becoming scarce. Further, there were present in American society, as in any complex society, certain forces that influenced the nature of social grouping of the various ethnic groups. Dahrendorf accounts for the formation of groups and classes in general by suggesting that the individual and his group encounters certain societal norms as well as sanctions which enforce these existing social principles, and that some individuals and groups do better than others in reaping society's rewards while others suffer certain punishments or negative sanctions depending upon the degree of conflict or similarity of the ethnic group with the physical environment and cultural norms that exist at the time of the immigrants' occupation of their new homeland. In Dahrendorf's words,

> The selection of norms always in-
> volves discrimination, not only
> against persons holding sociolog-
> ically random moral convictions,
> but also against social positions
> that may debar their incumbents
> from conformity with established
> values (quoted from Glazer and
> Moynihan, 1975, pp. 12-13).

This is not dissimilar to what M.G. Smith, following
Furnival, writes about the nature of pluralism in
Africa:

> ...the collective character, and
> the scope of its substantive
> differentiations, must be sufficent-
> ly rigorous and pervasive to estab-
> lish an effective order of corporate
> inequalities and subordination by
> the differential distribution of
> civil and political rights and the
> economic, social, and other oppor-
> tunities that these permit or
> enjoin (1969, op. cit., p. 430).

As these statements point out, those social positions
and work roles that were often accessible to the
immigrants, and in many cases to the succeeding
generations, were positions that were not endowed with
social status. In fact, many of these positions were
endowed with social stigma. This certainly had the
consequence of motivating many ethnic members to do
all they could to climb out of their original social
positions in a society that in fact encouraged its
members to engage in social mobility through the free
enterprise ideology of the capitalistic system. One
psychological orientation for initiating the process
of social mobility, which had considerable sociological
implications, was that of "anticipatory socialization"
(Merton, 1957, p. 265) where the ethnic members, or
certain of their number, identify with the out-group,
or with the dominant majority, in order to lubricate
the pathways of social mobility, maximize economic
gain, and create as much social and cultural distance
as possible from the stigma-producing environment of
immigrant ethnicity. At least in the American case it

is only after a few generations, after the various ethnic groups have won their status and have come to maintain a level of adaptation and integration in American society that, with this greater acceptance by the larger American society, and positive integration within the macrosystem, we find a turning back to what one never totally gave up, in order to reestablish what real American identity is in the first place: a heterogeneous mix of a variety of cultural identities synthesized (to some extent) into a (plausibly) adequately functioning personality which belongs to, identifies with, a number of differentiated and specialized roles and/or groups. Only after societal acceptance and integration with a certain modicum of acculturation on the part of all groups concerned does the force of ethnicity reassert itself, although in a different guise, in order to express certain needs, identities, and role requirements that press for gratification and actualization.

8.2. It is well established that the greater priority for ethnicity to reassert itself was in the political sphere, for the resurgence of ethnicity in the U.S., as in other societies, has largely functioned as an effective basis for political action. As Daniel Bell pointed out, the ethnic movement has taken a political form because of certain basic shifts in power and values within American society that has made ethnic identification an effective vehicle for social change (1975, p. 141). Bell enumerates several dominant trends in social change that have laid the groundwork for the recrudescence of ethnicity. I shall list them here (see Bell, 1975, pp.142-152):

1. Enlargement of the political boundaries and the political arena, which have come to include more and more individuals and wider networks involving a greater number of social groups in American society.

2. There has been an increase in the number of actors and claims in the political arena as a direct result of the first social trend.

3. Because of the greater inclusion of social groups there have also been challenges to the present day distribution of status and privilege, primarily by those who did not have fair access to society's rewards, but also by certain members of the upper

middle classes who championed the cause of the minorities.

4. Consequently, there has been a general questioning of dominant American norms and legitimations that in the past had maintained the status quo.

5. There has been a distinct tendency toward more inclusive identities, most importantly, political identities.

6. There has been a shift from market decisions to political decisions; or more accurately, there has occurred a politicization of economics and the organization of common interest groups with an attendant ideology of the communal society.

7. We have also seen a redefinition of the value of equality: equality of opportunity which can be defined as a non-zero-sum game, and equality of result which refers to a direct actual access to the resources and which is a zero-sum game. And it is within this zero-sum game that we find open political conflict and competition, and as well, an increase in the experience of relative deprivation that has been derived from the heightened expectations of the members in that political arena.

8. The onset and development of a post-industrial society resulted in the greater emphasis on skill, especially through education, and those without skills were left with little but political action in order to secure advancement.

9. There has been a general decline of authority in several spheres of American culture: in the status system, where a greater emphasis on egalitarianism has undermined the more authoritarian power pyramids of the older order of society; in the structure of organizational life, where we find fewer bosses and a greater independence of effort and guidance among the workers; in professional life, where there has been a marked lessening in elitism; and in general realms of cultural expression, where we have witnessed a lessening in the standards of judgement and respect for age, and where we have seen "the destruction of the idea of genre," the merging or disappearance of distinctive styles of cultural expression.

10. There has been a shift in American ideology with the development of Third World ideologies emphasizing anti-imperialism.

11. And lastly, Bell cites the growing recognition of the progressively dominant "external proletariat," a recognition of an international interdependence on workers from other, often distant cultural centers, where large numbers of migrated minorities find work in other urban centers and other countries which directly affect the growth of pluralism, and therefore, the significance of ethnicity in the urban centers of the world.

In sum, the greater mingling of peoples in the urban context generated the conditions for developing expanded identities formed along economic and political parameters. This, in turn, resulted in attenuated identities because of the relative lack of affective grounding for those reestablishing identities. The culture was changing and syncretizing, merging old ideas and social structures into new ones, which necessitated forms of social control that were best met by the further bureaucratization of social structures. This progressive rationalization of society undermined the affective grounding or older social structures based on familistic or particularistic principles, social structures such as primary networks of extended kin. Since the ethnic groups had always been based on such familistic principles, it was not farfetched to see how lost affective foundations for social life could be regained by politicizing the ethnic group in order to obtain the power to make decisions that would reestablish those lost principles of communal life.

8.3. Others have emphasized the importance of this affective component in the rise of the new ethnicity. In an earlier work, Glazer and Moynihan (1963) noted that the resurgence of ethnicity appeared to be related to the decline of occupational identity which had, for many, been a source of self-esteem, and the decline of religious identity which provided a familistic framework for wider social relations and ideology. Dashevsky adds alienation in mass society and rapid sociocultural change that led persons to seek out some source of symbolic security (1976, p. 4). And Parsons discusses the intensification of "groupism" in the face of rapid social change, anomic conditions, and alienation: "...the high emotional loading of the status of group membership and identity is one major type of reaction" (1975, p. 68). "...it may involve a more complex combination of potential and, to a certain degree, actual disruptive consequences for social solidarity and, at the same time, a kind of constructive mode of reintegration of population elements into structures which are less anomic and alienative than their members might otherwise be exposed to" (Ibid., p. 69). Kinton certainly agrees with Parsons in his statement that ethnic identity functions as a source of hope in avoiding the "lonely crowd" syndrome. For the older people the "ethnic revival" offers a political transformation with the "little guy" gaining control. And for the youth the new ethnicity serves as the peer group's reference point in school and in their leisure time pursuits. The active seeking of small group boundaries and patterns of differentiation from other unlike groups and the inscrutable masses is highly preferred to the alternative of a generalized national identity. This process Parsons calls "dedifferentiation:" This refers to a going back to something lost, the particularistic and the diffuse (op. cit. p. 69). General personal identity can often be, at least partially, recovered through the symbolically articulated ethnic group.

8.4. Glazer and Moynihan acknowledge this need for personal identity based on diffuse, affect-laden, particularistic ties. These sentiments are considered deep enough to be called "primordial." In their Introduction (1975, p. 3), Glazer and Moynihan account for one aspect of the importance of ethnicity in that ethnicity may express deeply felt, universally shared, human needs that have become diffused by the development of modern urban society* and refocused in recent times by certain political and social developments common to all who have experienced social pluralism.

*By this is meant industrialization, nucleated families, rationalization of religion, minority status, discrimination, and the scarcity and differential distribution of important and expected resources.

These primordial sentiments articulate themselves at one level through the cultural vehicle of honor. It is this sense of honor that may have been diffused, if not lost, through the process of modernization and industrialization. Max Weber pointed out the significance of honor in the context of ethnicity early in the development of modern sociology. In his words, the ethnic group has, as one of its bases, a certain "belief in a specific 'honor' of their members, not shared by outsiders, i.e., the sense of ethnic honor" (in Parsons and Shils, 1961, p. 307). "The sense of ethnic honor is a specific honor of the masses..., for it is accessible to anybody who belongs to the subjectively believed community of descent" (Ibid., p. 308). This sense of ethnic honor and ethnic identity is probably no better articulated and expressed than in rituals and ceremonials of the ethnic group.

> The sense of history is celebrated in collective ritual. Ritual acts are also expressions of commitment, be it to a religion, to a nation of loyal citizens, or to an ethnic group. Such acts are a collective experience that teaches those who participate who they are. The redundance of ritual goes beyond verbal expression by reinforcing emotional response. Participants identify with one another in the sharing of an explicit sense of purpose. Rituals of belonging are reaffirmations of origin, dramatizations of ancestral suffering and triumph, out of which future purpose is born and sustained (DeVos and Romanucci-Ross, 1975, p. 365).

DeVos and Romanucci-Ross are here referring to a relatively powerful cultural experience that certainly implies the existence of a sense of honor, emotional commitments to the group, and the inertia of group identity that will carry its members successfully through the gauntlet of the forces of assimilation and acculturation. But, we would question whether or not this reflects the "primordial" nature of ethnicity. The references to origins, ancestral suffering and triumph, and future purpose does appear to connote a

certain primordiality. But, these forms of ceremonial
may have been borne out of existential circumstances
which generated a need to believe in the fundamental
nature of ethnicity. In this regard, Fallers writes,

> The term "primordial" has been
> criticized on the ground that
> the social bonds and cultural
> unities in question are often
> not at all ancient, but on the
> contrary are demonstrably quite
> recent. For example, several
> million persons in Eastern
> Nigeria "discovered," with the
> help of ideologists, ethnographers
> and colonial administrators, that
> they were all Ibo only during the
> British colonial period. This new
> unity, however, once discovered,
> became very strong, forming the
> basis for the Biafran secession
> movement a few years after indepen-
> dence. "Material interests" of
> course become involved, as they do
> in such situations, but this does
> not alter the fact that the com-
> munity on behalf of which these
> interests were asserted had come
> to think of itself as a primordial
> one (italics original, from The
> Social Anthropology of the Nation-
> State 1974, p. 12, cited here from
> Stein and Hill, 1977, p. 42).

This African example can easily apply to American
ethnicity today, especially to America's white ethnic
groups. Contemporary American ethnicity is not
necessarily a phenomenon of deep lying ancestral
identities that press for reemergence, but rather
may be the manifestation of groups of individuals
making strategic choices as a means for gaining power
and privilege, for as Bell suggests (1975, p. 171),
without the need for political power and a sense of
influence the phenomenon of ethnicity could fade.

During the course of David Schneider's study of
American kinship (1968) he also found that the
content and functions of American ethnicity may be

quite different from what they were a generation or two earlier. In an informal memorandum to Talcott Parsons (quoted in Glazer and Moynihan, 1975) Schneider makes many cogent points about contemporary ethnicity in America, four of which are noted here:

1. Ethnic identity today is largely voluntary. It is not ascribed and enforced as it was among the immigrant and first generation Americans.

2. Ethnic identification and status is largely devoid of social content, i.e., traditional roles and institutions; the behaviorial patterns of the immigrant generation are not articulately adhered to today.

3. "The marks of identity are in a very important sense 'empty symbols'; symbols empty of elaborate social distinctions, and thus they are able to function freely and smoothly in this multi-ethnic social system while maintaining a distinct cultural-symbolic identity as markers" (Ibid., p. 65).

4. With the "desocialization" of American ethnic groups they are transformed into "primarily cultural-symbolic groups" (Ibid., p. 66), being voluntary and selective, and interest-oriented in the formation of networks of social solidarity. One significant function of this group solidarity formation is the intensification of feelings (Ibid., p. 67). The crucible of this new genre of ethnicity appears to be the marital or conjugal household. The continuity of old traditions is not really important. As Schneider has stated, "It does not require the learning of a totally new social role for the Irish girl to marry the Italian; they are both Catholic at least and she picks up some Italian, learns some cooking styles, and, lo, the symbolic identification is set" (Ibid., p. 65). The requirement, then, for establishing a foundation for the intensification of feeling is the formation of a common cultural base-line or orientation within the conjugal household that allows the acceptance and sharing of a common framework for experience. This adaptive strategy appears to be very important in a society where an increasing number of mates and spouses come from different ethnic backgrounds.

49

8.5. A common ethnic cultural orientation in the conjugal household provides a greater sense of psychological, social and cultural boundaries. This experience of boundedness can then be generalized to progressively larger social structures identifying with the same ethnicity which itself becomes a definition of boundary. The social structure, on any level, focuses problems, articulates sentiments, and generates oppositions which press for resolutions. In their discussion on the functionality of social boundaries LeVine and Campbell maintain that boundedness of a social group more easily achieves a functioning network of reciprocal obligations (1972, p. 110). The formation of structures in the development of adaptive forms usually operates in terms of the principle of least effort or the maximization of efficiency. Within a political evolutionary framework, LeVine and Campbell state that "Sharply bounded political organizations displace ones with unstable or unclear boundaries through the selective propagation of adaptive forms" (Ibid., p. 111). It is more efficient "if boundaries of different types coincide rather than overlap, and functional efficiency of group coordination...is improved when it is clear who belongs to the group and who does not" (Ibid., p. 111).

The importance of boundedness in social and political effectiveness is attested to by Abner Cohen in his study of power and symbolism:

> Ethnicity is fundamentally a political phenomenon, as the symbols of the traditional culture are used as mechanisms for the articulation of political alignments....
>
> Ethnicity provides an array of symbolic strategies for solving most or all of the basic problems of organizational articulation. The cultural identity of the group provides the major mechanism for distinctiveness. The tendency for the ethnic group to be highly endogamous distinguishes the group further in creating an exclusive network of... relationships and thereby enclosing a great deal of primary relationships

50

within the group and inhibiting the formation of such relationships with people from outside the group. Even when the group goes through a process of change, it will adjust to the new situation in terms of its own traditional customs without adopting customs shared with members of other groups. The dense network of kinship and affinity created by endogamous marriages within the group will enhance the distinctiveness of the group further by transforming it into a 'bilateral descent group', whose members can claim sharing a common 'origin' or being from 'the same stock'.

These symbols of distinctiveness will serve at the same time as channels for communication. They will also help in articulating an authority structure by mobilizing an informal authority agency. Similarly, the hierarchies within religious congregations and organs for welfare and mutual help can become vehicles for routinization of decision making procedures. The symbols providing these organizational mechanisms are ideologically integrated within such mottoes as 'our customs are different', the sacredness of our traditions', and so on. The ideology is further elaborated to cover a narrative 'historical' account of the origin, the goings and comings of the group. Finally, through the continual observance of the customs and ceremonies peculiar to the group, the members are continually socialized in the culture of the group (1974, pp. 97-98).

Cohen's statement provides us with a good sense of the

pervasive importance of ethnicity for the individual, for the group, and for the total society whose destiny, in considerable measure, can be shaped by the structure and dynamics of ethnic groups and ethnic cultures within that society. In this sense the functions and dynamics of ethnicity have sociocultural evolutionary significance.

8.6. The problem of urban adaptation that most immigrants faced and weathered provided a common context of experience in which to forge new adaptive strategies for survival, for social mobility, and for cultural development. Those developments matured over a few generations and emerged as sociocultural movements of the 1960's and 1970's. Since many of the larger social groups in the pluralistic urban centers were ethnic groups, it is not difficult to see why ethnicity became the basis for social movements and "a cultural mode for economic and political advancement" (Bell, 1975, p. 172). Daniel Bell has distinguished basically two kinds of social movements: First, the symbolic expressive movement which is made up of affective ties and consists of such groups as the V.F.W., Masons, and other sorts of fraternal organizations; or, on the other hand, symbolic expressive movements may be the social action type of affective solidarity and consist of such groups as the Weathermen, S.D.S., or the Women's and Gay Lib groups. The second kind of social movement is instrumental and based in ties of common material interest with little or no affective ties manifested. Instrumental aims are usually very narrowly conceived and once the goal is reached the social unit's function subsides. But, there are problems with both types of groups involved in their respective kinds of movements:

> ...the problem for symbolic expressive groups is that while they can be mobilized quickly in periods of stress and peak experience, without a sustained, continuing interest which is real, and which has tangible payoffs for the members, the movements burn themselves out. The problem for instrumental organizations is the need to readapt themselves to new purposes when the old goals have become realized (Bell, 1975, p. 165).

52

It is Bell's thesis that the most highly effective social units that could propagate a powerful social movement would consist in a combination of symbolic expressive and instrumental orientations. American ethnic groups and the ethnicity movement, with its multi-level functionality, is one prime example of Bell's thesis.

Although a considerable amount of attention has been given to the phenomenon of ethnicity, relatively little attention has been given to ethnicity as a social movement. Furthermore, in a great proportion of studies that have formulated functional interpretations of ethnicity we find that the positive, eufunctional, therapeutic aspects of ethnicity have been stressed. Relatively little attention has been given to the negative functions of ethnicity in general and virtually nothing has been done on the pathological aspects of the ethnicity movement in particular; most of the literature on this new ethnicity being dominated by writers who are ethnophiles. To date, one study stands out which focuses on the dysfunctions, the anti-therapeutic or regressive functions of ethnicity and the New Ethnicity Movement: The Ethnic Imperative (1971) by Stein and Hill is a study that employs a psychoanalytic anthropological theoretical perspective to examine the nature and development of the New White Ethnic Movement. This movement is compared to what anthropologists have recognized as nativistic, millenarian, or crisis cult movements which are reactions of oppressed groups of people throughout the world who have experienced increased relative deprivation, loss of status, downward mobility, disillusionment, and little hope for realistic and satisfying gains in the foreseeable future.

The precursor of white ethnic disillusionment was the American Dream that so many white ethnics worked so hard toward through at least two generations. The promise of social mobility, prosperity, a sense of achievement, and an expectation that their children would further their assimilation and supplement their wealth and status appeared to have become greatly attenuated during the course of events of the late 1960's and 1970's. The liberationist movements of sex, drugs, and politics produced a reaction from the white parochial Catholic ethnic groups; and the assassinations of J. F. Kennedy, Martin Luther King Jr., and shortly thereafter, R. F. Kennedy, seemed to throw the ethnic working people of America into cultural and psychological turmoil which was not easily corrected.

In the words of Stein and Hill:

> In Robert Kennedy was united the symbol and actuality of an inte-grated nation. With his assassina-tion during the summer of 1968, the symbolism of the American Dream literally disintegrated. The empha-sis is not a mere play on words, but gets to the heart of what integration and its precipitous fragmentation mean. The dream was now in pieces; the idealism was now shattered; and the fragmented and rage ridden Amer-ican culture was ripe for exploita-tion by those who lived and led others by fear and hate. Many of those who would have voted for Kennedy voted for Wallace in the 1968 presidential campaign (1971, p. 116).

The disappointments were followed by a high level of discontent that was expressed in the form of crises as seen in civil disobedience, riots, and a host of new religious movements that sprung up all over the country.

> ...only in the context of the collapse of a cultural consensus (identity) are we able to under-stand the simultaneous and acute eruptions of discontent that are frequently called "crises": the crisis of confidence, the crisis in the classroom, the crisis on the campus, the crisis in the cities, the crisis of identity, the crisis of idealism, and the "generation gap" (Ibid., p. 114).

And, to add to the difficulty of the ethnic working class were uncontrollable events that were perceived to work against them: legislation that allowed the nonworking brown peoples to live off the taxes of the white ethnics' salaries, inflation that allowed less and less material rewards and made it more and more difficult for the children of white ethnics to secure a college education that was their one sure path into the mainstream of American culture, and now the revolutionary ideologies of the 1960's seemed to have no direction or leadership. The consequence was reaction. "The New Ethnicity will be seen as one means among many current attempts to reorder personal and social reality based on a pervasive sense of inner and outer disorder" (Ibid., p. 11) "...as middle-aging revolutionaries repudiate their earlier reformist positions and turn to the extremism of reaction, the ideologies and programs of which for one 'final solution' or another are embraced by those identities are likewise threatened" (Ibid., p. 115). "The new ethnic identity is the search for pre-ambivalent roots, certitude, and security" (Ibid. p. 115).

The upheavals of the 1960's, then established conditions of reaction in the 1970's that created in many a readiness for a new ideology that would appeal to their needs that arose from their anxieties:

> The readiness--a readiness common
> to all revitalized identities--is
> based not on the sudden awareness
> of continuity with an ethnic past,
> but on the realization of discon-
> tinuity with the American future
> in which one had invested so high-
> ly. It is the very romanticization
> of ethnicity that is the key to the
> alienation from the past that the
> New Ethnics redress by the inver-
> sion of values and the merger of
> self with group (Ibid., p. 43).

The new cultural configuration is based not on historical tradition mainly, but on certain selected aspects of the traditions that are organized to adapt the group to their changed (as they perceived it) life conditions and restore order, establish a modicum of predictability, and bring a sense of self-esteem and a sense of importance to their lives. Self-hate, self-doubt, disillusionment, and downward status-mobility must be brought under control through a separation from mainstream America and a reevaluation of values. In the words of Stein and Hill:

> ...the identity, ideology and imagery of the New Ethnicity is far from indigenous, but is predicated on opposition to aspects of American culture with which it defines itself by contrast. The identity of the New Ethnicity is not independent of American identity. It requires, however, the externalized enemy to create and perpetuate the new internal solidarity. What is within the personal and group boundary is systematically related to what is outside that boundary (Ibid., pp. 10-11).

The distinctive features of the New Ethnicity are those that

> systematically relate to the oppositional process: the placing of feeling over mind or reason, past over present, collectivity over individuality; the Balkanization of politics and culture...the gerrymandering of ethnicity in education; a racist reinterpretation of American culture history in which all social ills are traced to the WASP; the rejection of American standards and their replacement with ethnic standards, an extolling of the virtues of the organic ethnic community without noticing its constrictions and coercions; the perception of modernization, urbanization, and future-orientation as

> negative and destructive; and the
> mystique of Volkstum. ...the
> creation of a new origin myth
> according to which the white
> ethnic past...emerges as equal
> or superior to American cul-
> ture. The origin myth serves
> as a charter for social action,
> creating a symbolic language
> of harmony within the movement
> and serving as a language of
> argument with the antagonistic
> world beyond (Ibid., pp. 161-162).

This oppositional process and the dichotomizing of
aspects of American mainstream and ethnic culture
according to positive and negative values is actually
an attempt to resolve a fundamental ambivalence
consisting of the cherishing of established American
ideals and mainstream culture and feelings of self-
abnegation, hostility born of the frustrations of
not attaining those ideals, and the identity of a
low-status out-group in relation to the perceived
WASP mainstream culture. The resolution is attempted
through the mechanism of projection and displacement:

> ...the conflict between the New
> Ethnic nativism and Americanization/
> assimilation ideology is not merely
> between ingroup and outgroup, but
> is a fundamental ambivalence within
> the nativist ingroup that is re-
> solved through the projection and
> displacement of rage and hostility
> into a stereotyped outgroup (the
> WASP) who now bares all the
> opprobrium of what was formerly
> self-hatred (Ibid., p. 161).

But, this mode of adaptation of huddling together has
its dysfunctional consequences in that it does not
ameliorate the conditions that the ethnic groups
reacted against:

> Ethnicity is one salve for
> modern wounds of violated and
> vulnerable identities. The

57

romanticized and idealized 'idols
of the tribe,' as Harold Isaacs
calls ethnicity [in Glazer and
Moynihan, 1975], not only create
security and safety from the hostile, alienating world outside,
but instill deeper fear of that
world. Hence the greater need
for the mystical womb of ethnos.
A vicious cycle is created
wherein ego, self, family,
neighborhood, and ethnic group
become more withdrawn and fear-
ful. The tribal cave, ideological and territorial, inspires
the very dread it assuages.
The feelings of belonging and
loyalty on the inside are in-
separable from the fears of
isolation and vulnerability on
the outside. The opposites are
symbiotically linked with one
another. Defense not only defends, but perpetuates the uncertainty and anxiety that require constant vigilance.
Defense must maintain what it
defends against. Ethnicity,
though, is only one among
increasingly diverse responses
to a generalized cultural con-
dition (Ibid., pp. 119-120).

Not only is the social group a defensive unit, es-
pousing a siege mentality, but the personality system
itself is highly defensive; repressing impulse life
and personal features that are unacceptable (such as
hatred and the need to express violence--not to men-
tion sexuality), choosing only those aspects of personality that fit the ideology that one is committed to,
projecting the repudiated characteristics onto out-
groups who can then become the targets of scapegoating
and rationalization for one's own "underprivileged"
predicament. In externalizing the threat there arises
the need to have external controls in the form of
authoritarian leadership which would rid the country
of its ills by separating out the bad people from the
good and giving the good people their due.

The dysfunctional characteristics of ethnic identity then include 1) "one-dimensional" individuality--one's ethnicity is everything, 2) ritualized obsessiveness about one's ethnic identity, 3) a high emotionality ("hypercathexis") of ethnic identity as a means of compensating for perceived faults in one's self-image, 4) an identity that is closed off to further growth, and 5) the "obliteration of individual distinctiveness" (Ibid., p. 7, quoting Devereux, in DeVos and Romanucci-Ross, 1975, p. 65). Although Stein and Hill acknowledge the positive attributes and potential ethnicity has in political affairs as well as psychologically in helping one to acknowledge one's ethnic characteristics (as opposed to hiding from them), they nevertheless maintain that the New Ethnic Movement has neurotic ramifications.

> We would evaluate ethnic identity, or any expression of identity, by the quality of humanness it evinces. With Devereux, we would emphasize that one cannot affirm one's humanness without concurrently confirming the humanness of others. Functional identity is inclusive; dysfunctional identity, which utilizes hysterical, paranoid, and dissociative defenses to maintain rigid boundaries, is exclusive. It is dysfunctional identity which we find at the core of the identity and ideology of the New Ethnicity (Ibid., p. 7). Yet, man's functionally relevant dissimilarity from all others is what makes him human: similar to others precisely through his high degree of differentiation. It is this which permits him to claim a human identity (Ibid., p. 7).

> Any distinction between authentic and inauthentic identity lies in the extent to which identity is based on genuine relation and insight, or pseudo-relation and self-conning, respectively. With

the former goes humility, and with
the latter, a terror-ridden arro-
gant pride (Ibid., p. 9).

Stein and Hill see recent American culture history as
periods in dialectical opposition. Individual persons
are often caught in the bind of living in both
cultural periods and unable to sort out the opposing
psycho-cultural influences that exist within the
person. The result very often is an identity crisis
which, in one form or another, begs for resolution.
"Each age is lived in dialectical relation to those
preceding it, embodying its spirit even as it repudiated it and replaced it with a new, and more pure,
spirit. Every present is a way of coping with the
past" (Ibid., p. 52).

In this section I have attempted to show how
the structure of ethnicity mobilizes power, generates
a resource base and facilitates a system for distribut-
ing the resources, both material and intangible, to
the members of that structure. The sociopolitical
dynamics of ethnicity elevates the status of the group
in the context of the larger society and maintains a
sense of honor that binds its members to each other
and to the cultural principles associated with the
group. The cultural symbols of ethnicity provide
the members with a feeling of continuity, belonging,
familiarity, commitment, and reciprocal obligations
which perpetuate the general aims and ideals of the
group. For the individual, ethnicity provides a
context for affective expressiveness of one's
distinctive ethnic culture and identity, attenuates
the experience of relative deprivation (or heightens
it if the goals and expectations have not been fully
met), and provides a social security system for those
members who make up that group. On the other hand,
the manifestation of ethnicity as a social ideological
movement may involve psychosocial dynamics that have
been unsuccessful in dealing with threatening sociocultural forces, consequently deepening their problems,
most of which lie beyond their awareness and their
capacity to comprehend.

PART III

CONCLUSION

SUMMATION AND CONCLUSIONS

In this paper I have constructed an analytical framework with which ethnicity can be conceived and researched. The concept of ethnicity is traced through six general theoretical parameters. The configuration of these parameters provide for a structural functional systems approach to the understanding of ethnicity.

The first parameter is the <u>environment</u> of ethnicity. This includes three subareas: a) the macrostructure of American culture and institutions, b) trends of change in American society and Western civilization, and c) the specific forces of assimilation.

The second parameter is the <u>levels of operation</u> of ethnicity which include three: a) the level of social structure or the organization of formal and informal relationships, b) the cultural level of symbolic expressivity, and c) the personality level of psychodynamics and adaptation.

The third parameter is the <u>set of components</u> of ethnicity manifested at the three levels of operation. The components are a host of features including the following: a certain degree of ethnocentrism, familistic-oriented relationships, a high degree of shared physical traits and cultural patterns, a certain degree of interactional intensity within a "communication field," pattern continuity in self-image, reference group identity, and physical proximity, ascribed minority status, a sense of ethnic honor, distinctive art forms and other cultural features that focus ethnicity and mobilize ethnic sentiment, history, and destiny.

The fourth parameter is the set of <u>models of the process of ethnic identity change</u>. These models include a) the configuration of macrostructural forces present in society that act upon the direction and dynamics of ethnic identity change, b) the cyclic model of Hansen, c) the assimilation stage model of Glaser, d) the functional adaptation model of Greeley, e) the communication-of-cultural-experience model of Nahirny and Fishman, and f) the crisis cult movement model of Stein and Hill.

The fifth parameter is the cause/function set. The subset of causes include migrations for labor, discrimination, differential power and status in the general society, shifts in power and values toward more egalitarian forms of social organization and modes of thinking, a growing ideology of anti-imperialism, inclusive identification on a national level, the decline of centralized and focused authority, increased mingling of different peoples, sociocultural conditions of anomie, and a highly rationalized and bureaucratized society that generated an increased emotional loading of groupism. The subset of functions include the salience of providing an efficient sociopolitical structure that has adaptability against contravening forces of society and that provides an array of symbolic strategies for the political mobilization and political alignments of individuals and groups; satisfies the need for small group boundaries, shores up a shaky personal identity by serving as an identity-marker and a structure for personality functioning, provides affect-laden ties maintaining a sense of honor and morale, is the focus for the reenactment of ritual and ceremony, provides a meaning system of orientation, maintains a conservative family organization through endogamous networks of relationships, maintains effective channels of communication, articulates an authority structure based on kinship and religion, provides a field and network for social assistance, is a vehicle for social movements, and can function as a culturally-constituted ego-defense mechanism for the adaptation to mass identity anxiety.

The sixth general theoretical parameter of ethnicity is the set of functional modes or types of ethnicity which are three: a) immigrant based orthodoxy, b) assimilated and adapted ethnicity, and c) the crisis cult style movement based on identity foreclosure and cultural reaction.

Ethnicity can be seen as a highly structured, multi-level human phenomenon with multi-functional significance. What can be said of ethnicity in particular can be said of culture in general. Therefore, we can conceive of ethnicity from the perspective of sociocultural evolution in that it has a considerable range and depth of adaptive significance and appears to figure in the irreversible forces of change for large populations in different parts of the world.

REFERENCES

Barth, Frederik 1969. Ethnic Groups and Boundaries: The Social Organization of Culture Differences. Boston: Little Brown.

Bell, Daniel 1975. "Ethnicity and Social Change" In Glazer and Moynihan, eds., Ethnicity: Theory and Experience. Cambridge: Harvard University Press.

Cohen, Abner 1974. Two Dimensional Man: An Essay on the Anthropology of Power and Symbolism. Berkeley and Los Angeles: University of California Press.

---- ---- 1974. Urban Ethnicity. ASA Monograph No. 12, London, N.Y.: Barnes and Nobel.

Dashevsky, Arnold, ed. 1976. Ethnic Identity in Society. N.Y.: Rand McNally.

Despres, Leo, ed. 1975. Ethnicity and Resource Competition in Plural Societies. Chicago: Aldine.

De Vos, George and Romanucci-Ross, Lola, eds. 1975. Ethnic Identity: Cultural Continuities and Change. Palo Alto: Mayfield.

Fallers, Lloyd 1974. The Social Anthropology of the Nation-State. Chicago: Aldine.

Geertz, Clifford 1963. "The Integrative Revolution: Primordial Sentiments and Civil Politics in the New States" In Geertz, ed. Old Societies and New States. Glencoe, Illinois: The Free Press.

Glaser, Daniel 1958. "Dynamics of Ethnic Identification" American Sociological Review, 1:31-40.

Glazer, Nathan 1954. "Ethnic Groups in America" In Freedom and Control in Modern Society, M. Berger, T. Abel, and C. Page, eds. N.Y.: Van Nostrand.

REFERENCES (CONTINUED)

Glazer, N. and Moynihan, D. 1963. Beyond the Melting Pot: The Negroes, Puerto Ricans, Jews, Italians, and Irish of New York City. Cambridge: MIT Press.

Glazer, N. and Moynihan D., eds. 1975. Ethnicity: Theory and Experience. Cambridge: Harvard University Press.

Gordon, Milton 1964. Acculturation in American Life. N.Y.: Oxford University Press.

Greeley, Andrew 1971. Why Can't They Be Like Us? N.Y.: E.P. Dutton.

---- ---- 1974. Ethnicity in the United States: A Preliminary Reconnaissance. N.Y.: Wiley and Sons Interscience.

Hansen, Marcus Lee 1937. The Problem of the Third Generation Immigrant. Rock Island, Illinois: The Augustana Historical Society.

Henry, Frances, ed. 1976. Ethnicity in the Americas. Chicago: Aldine.

Hughes, Charles 1976. Custom-Made: Introductory Readings in Cultural Anthropology, 2nd edition. Chicago: Rand McNally.

Isajiw, Wsevolod 1974. "Definitions of Ethnicity" Ethnicity 1:111-124.

Kinton, Jack 1977. American Ethnic Revival: Group Pluralism Entering America's Third Century. Aurora, Illinois: Social Science and Sociological Resources.

LeVine, Robert and Campbell, Donald 1972. Ethnocentrism: Theories of Conflict, Ethnic Attitudes and Group Behavior. N.Y.: John Wiley & Sons.

Merton, Robert 1957. Social Theory and Social Structure. Glencoe: The Free Press.

REFERENCES (CONTINUED)

Nahirny, V. and Fishman, J. 1965. "American
 Immigrant Groups: Ethnic Identification and
 the Problem of Generations" Sociological
 Review, 13:311-326.

Novak, Michael 1972. The Rise of the Unmeltable
 Ethnics. N.Y.: MacMillan and Co.

Parsons, T. and Shils, E., et. al. 1961. Theories
 of Society vol. 1. Glencoe, Illinois: The
 Free Press.

Schermerhorn, Richard 1949. These Our People.
 Boston: Heath and Co.

---- ---- 1970. Comparative Ethnic Relations: A
 Framework for Theory and Research. N.Y.:
 Random House.

Schneider, D.M. 1969. American Kinship: A Cultural
 Account. Englewood Cliffs, N.D.: Prentice Hall.

Shils, Edward 1957. "Primordial, Personal, Sacred,
 and Civil Ties" British Journal of Sociology
 8:130-145.

Smith, M.G. 1969. "Some Developments in the Analytic
 Framework of Pluralism" In Leo Kuper and M.G.
 Smith, Eds., Pluralism in Africa. Los Angeles:
 University of California Press.

Sowell, Thomas, ed. 1978. Essays and Data on
 American Ethnic Groups. Washington D.C.:
 The Urban Institute.

Stein, H. and Hill, R. 1977. The Ethnic Imperative.
 University Park and London: Pennsylvania State
 University Press.

Weber, Max 1961. "The Ethnic Group" In Parsons and
 Shils, et. al., eds., Theories of Society vol. 1
 Glencoe, Illinois: The Free Press.

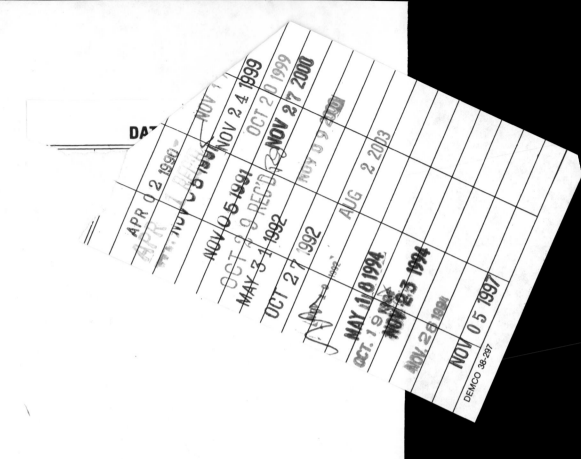